AMAZING JOURN

D0635143

To the Depths of the Ocean

Rod Theodorou

Heinemann
LIBRARY

www.heinemann.co.uk/library
Visit our website to find out more information about Heinemann Library books.

To order:
Phone 44 (0) 1865 888112
Send a fax to 44 (0) 1865 314091
Visit the Heinemann bookshop at www.heinemann.co.uk/library to browse our catalogue and order online.

First published in Great Britain by Heinemann Library, Halley Court, Jordan Hill, Oxford OX2 8EJ, part of Harcourt Education.
Heinemann is a registered trademark of Harcourt Education Ltd.

© Harcourt Education Ltd 2000, 2006
Second edition first published in paperback in 2007
The moral right of the proprietor has been asserted.

All rights reserved. No part of this publication may be reproduced, stored in a retrieval system, or transmitted in any form or by any means, electronic, mechanical, photocopying, recording, or otherwise, without either the prior written permission of the publishers or a licence permitting restricted copying in the United Kingdom issued by the Copyright Licensing Agency Ltd, 90 Tottenham Court Road, London W1T 4LP (www.cla.co.uk).

Editorial: Clare Lewis
Design: Victoria Bevan, Michelle Lisseter, and Bridge Creative Services
Illustrations: Stephen Lings and Jane Pickering at Linden Artists
Picture Research: Hannah Taylor
Production: Helen McCreath

Printed in China

13 digit ISBN 978 0 431 05651 7 (hardback)
10 09 08 07 06
10 9 8 7 6 5 4 3 2 1

13 digit ISBN 978 0 431 05762 0 (paperback)
11 10 09 08 07
10 9 8 7 6 5 4 3 2 1

British Library Cataloguing in Publication Data
Theodorou, Rod and Telford, Carole
Amazing journeys: To the depths of the ocean – 2nd edition
577.7
A full catalogue record for this book is available from the British Library.

Acknowledgements
The publishers would like to thank the following for permission to reproduce photographs:
BBC: Jeff Rotman p.**16**; NHPA: Norbert Wu, p.**10**, p.**21**, p.**23**; Oxford Scientific Films: David B Fleetman p.**15**, Doug Allan p.**23**, Gerard Soury p.**18**, Howard Hall p.**11**, p.**13**, p.**19**, Kathie Atkinson p.**11**, Ken Smith Laboratory/Scripps p.**25**, Liz Bomford p.**27**, Norbert Wu p.**17**, p.**21**, Paul Kay p.**23**, Peter Parks p.**13**, p.**20**, Steve Early p.**15**; Science Photo Library: NASA p.**6**, Peter Ryan/Scripps p.**24**.
Opposite: Bruce Coleman Collection.

Cover photograph of an octopus, reproduced with permission of Alamy Images/Jeff Rotman.

Every effort has been made to contact copyright holders of any material reproduced in this book. Any omissions will be rectified in subsequent printings if notice is given to the publishers.

The paper used to print this book comes from sustainable resources.

MORAY COUNCIL LIBRARIES & INFO.SERVICES

20 21 59 22	
Askews	
J577.7	

Contents

Introduction	*6*
Journey map	*8*
At the surface	*10*
The teeming shallows	*12*
The continental shelf	*14*
The twilight zone	*16*
Deep water giants	*18*
Into the darkness	*20*
At the ocean floor	*22*

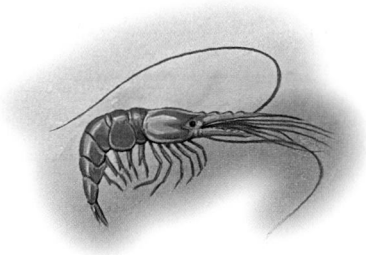

The sulphur vents *24*

Conservation and the future *26*

Glossary *28*

Find out more *30*

Index *32*

Some words are shown in bold letters, **like this**. You can find out what these words mean by looking in the Glossary.

Introduction

You are about to go on an amazing journey. You are going to climb inside a **submersible**, an advanced mini-submarine, and be lowered off a ship into the swelling waters of the Pacific Ocean. Millions of animals live beneath the waves, each one specially adapted to survive in this hostile environment.

You will begin your journey amongst glittering silver **shoals** of fish, pursued by fast **lone** hunters. Then you are going to descend into the gloomy depths to view an amazing alien environment. You will see incredible creatures, huge **predators**, and witness animals unknown to science until very recently.

With the help of a submersible like this you are about to explore the depths of the mighty Pacific Ocean.

Viewed from space Earth looks like the "blue planet". Over 70 per cent of its surface is covered by seawater. These oceans are the most unexplored places on Earth. Most are over 4,000 metres (13,000 feet) deep. Only the first 200 metres (655 feet) of the water is warm and lit by the sun. The rest is dark and cold, but not lifeless.

Some parts of the ocean are incredibly deep. America's Grand Canyon is a spectacular land **gorge** over 1,600 metres (5,200 feet) deep. Compare this to the deepest part of the Pacific Ocean (the Marianas Trench) which is nearly 11,000 metres (36,000 feet) deep! What kind of creatures could survive in these freezing depths?

The submersible's hatch is closing. You are about to find out.

The world's five oceans.

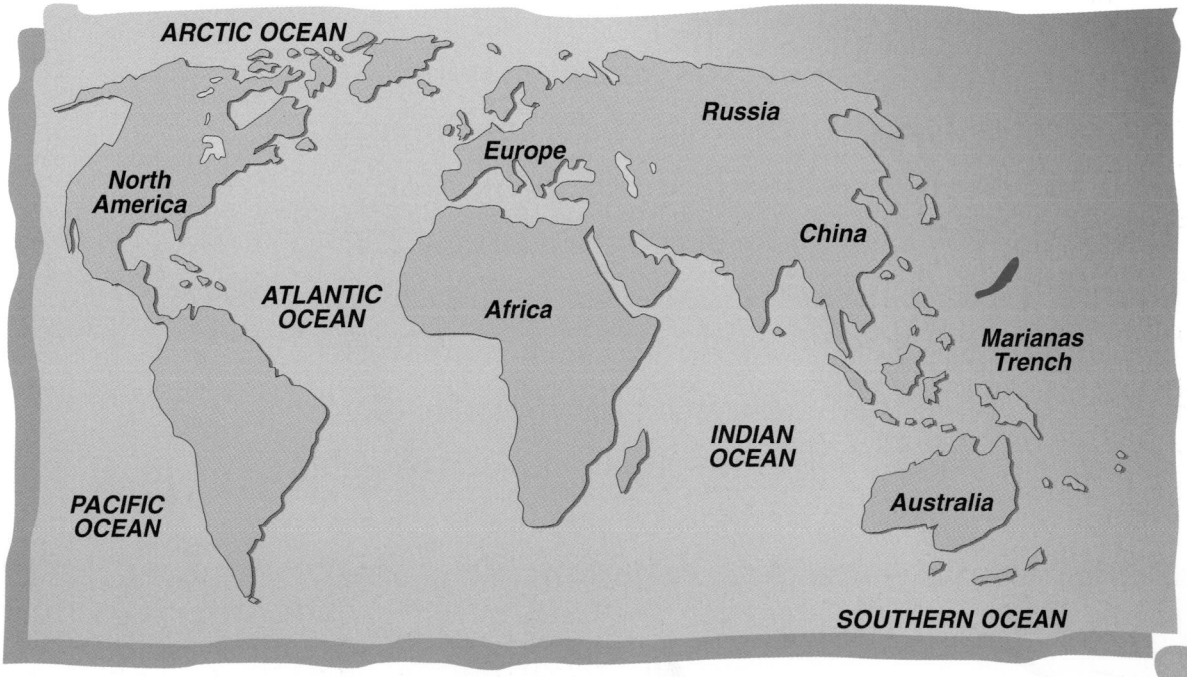

Journey map

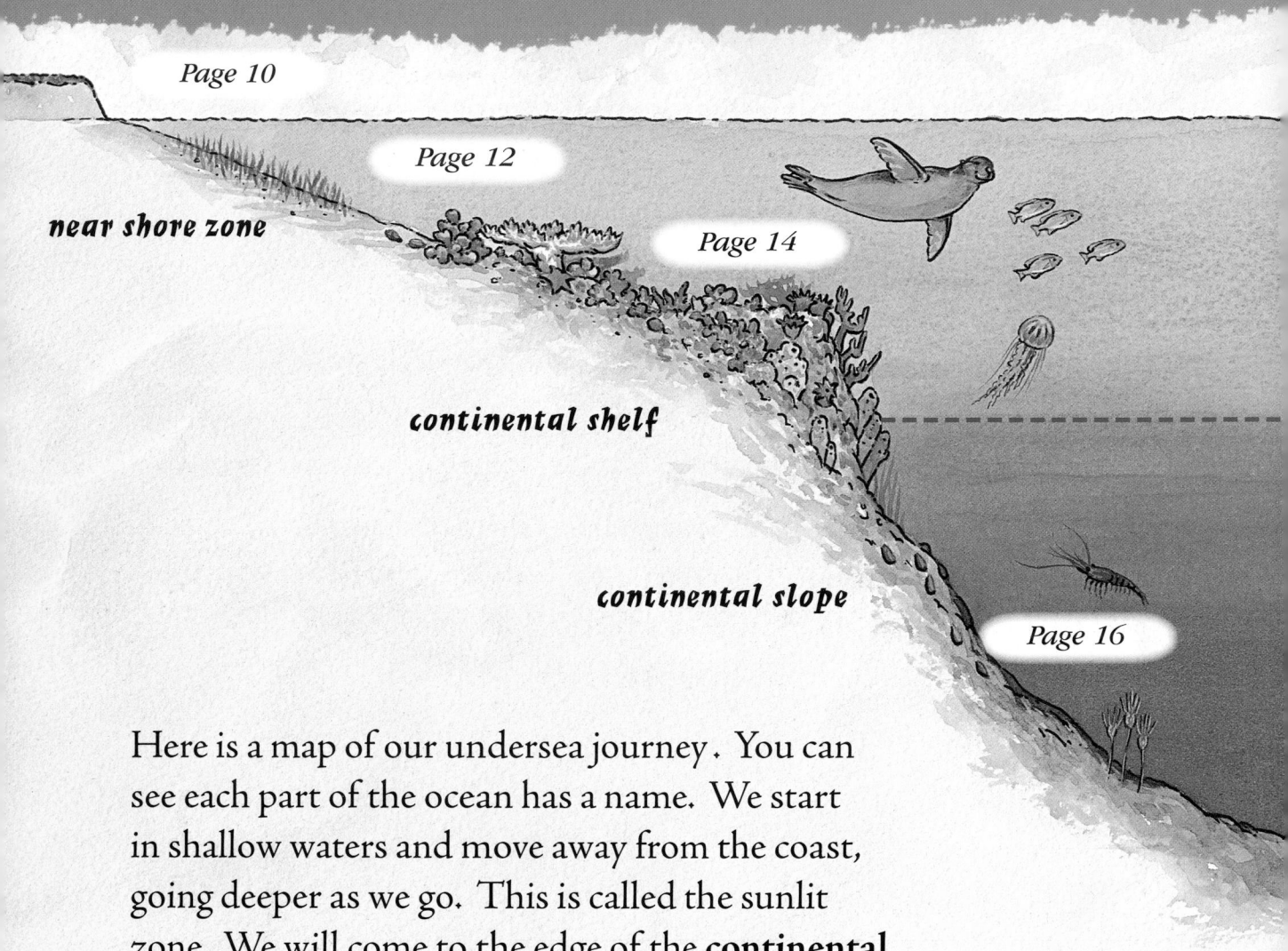

Here is a map of our undersea journey. You can see each part of the ocean has a name. We start in shallow waters and move away from the coast, going deeper as we go. This is called the sunlit zone. We will come to the edge of the **continental shelf** and drop down into the deep, open ocean. The sunlight cannot shine deeper than about 200 metres (650 feet). These gloomy waters are called the twilight zone. By the time we reach the 1,000-metre (3,300-foot) mark it will be completely black outside the **porthole** window. We will need to turn our **submersible's** lights on to see any life as we sink further down towards the very bottom of the ocean.

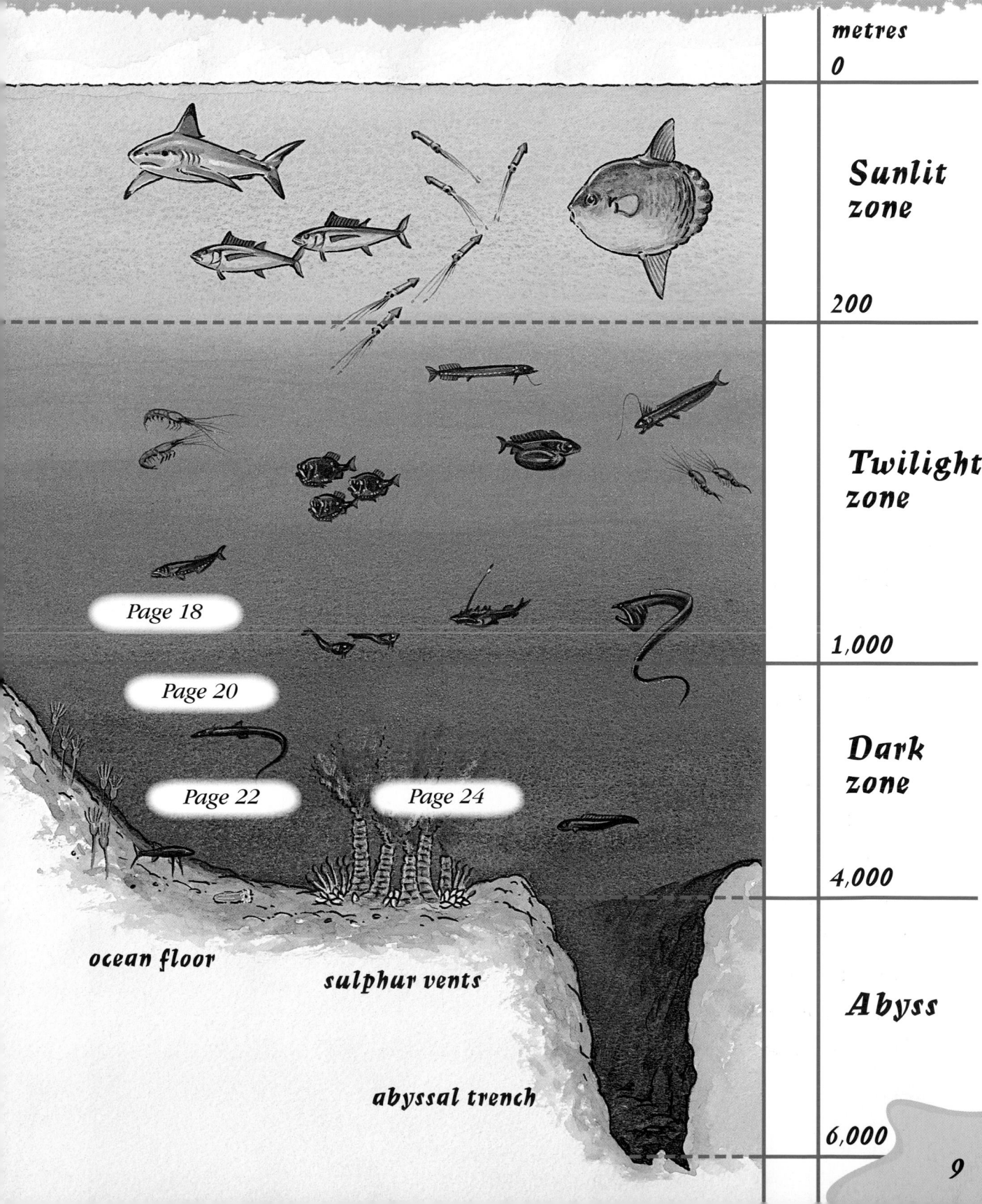
metres
0
Sunlit zone
200
Twilight zone
1,000
Dark zone
4,000
Abyss
6,000
Page 18
Page 20
Page 22
Page 24
ocean floor
sulphur vents
abyssal trench

At the surface

As the **submersible** is lowered over the side of our ship we have one last look at the sky and waves. Gulls and a **lone** albatross soar overhead. Frightened by some undersea **predator,** we are lucky enough to see a huge manta ray leap out of the water. Tiny flying fish also break the surface and glide above the wave crests before disappearing again. With a loud thud the submersible smacks into the sea and in a burst of bubbles we sink beneath the surface. The dolphins that have been following our ship soon come to investigate. Bright sunlight glints off the silver fish that pass by in large **shoals**. There is life all around us.

The "wings" of a huge manta ray break the surface of the water.

Portuguese man o'war

This is actually a **colony** of smaller animals that live together. One is a large gas-filled float which sticks up above the surface and acts like a sail, moving the colony along. Others are stinging **tentacles** that catch food.

Sailfish

This fast hunter has a streamlined body built for speed. It can swim at an amazing 109 kilometres (68 miles) per hour, faster than a cheetah can run!

Flying fish

When a predator chases the flying fish it gathers speed and then jumps out of the water. It spreads out its large fins, which act like wings, carrying the flying fish through the air for about 30 seconds.

The teeming shallows

Many of the fish we see in the sunlit zone are dark green-blue on the top and silver underneath. This makes it hard for them to be seen by **predators** from above (looking downwards at the green-blue depths) or below (looking up at the silvery surface).

Invisible to our eyes are millions of tiny **plankton**. The plant-plankton grow in the warm sunlight, whilst the animal-plankton feed on them, and on other tiny food **particles** that are blown towards the ocean's surface by storms or undersea **currents**. Smaller fish feast on this plankton. Larger fish eat the smaller fish. Even giant whales eat the plankton, and other tiny shrimps called krill. Without the plankton most other ocean life would die.

1 *ocean sunfish*
2 *skipjack tuna*
3 *manta ray*
4 *Pacific sardine*
5 *common dolphin*
6 *blue shark*
7 *cod*
8 *dolphin fish*
9 *krill*
10 *Pacific right whale*
11 *basking shark*

The shallow water is lit up by the Sun's rays and is full of life.

Plankton

Plankton are microscopic creatures. Some are tiny plants. Others are tiny animals that eat this plant-plankton. Some are fish **fry** or the tiny **larvae** of other sea animals.

Whale shark

At 18 metres (60 feet) long this is the largest fish in the world. It is completely harmless and wanders the ocean alone, feeding on plankton.

Pacific salmon

Salmon are born in freshwater streams and then **migrate** to the sea. They live in the ocean for several years before travelling huge distances back to the streams where they were born. Here they **spawn**, and then die.

The continental shelf

The **submersible** dives deeper. We can't see the ocean surface any more, but the temperature **gauge** indicates the water is still warm (15°C / 59°F) and there is still a lot of light. We catch sight of the seabed below us. We are now at the **continental shelf**.

The submersible's whining **propeller** blades slow down for a while as we stop to enjoy the life around us. A green turtle flaps slowly by on its way to feed on turtle grass, a kind of seaweed. Before us we can see the end of the continental shelf. Soon we will have to go over that cliff-edge and descend down the steep continental slope into deeper, darker waters.

1 *coral*
2 *sponges*
3 *seaweed*
4 *green turtle*
5 *barracuda*
6 *jellyfish*
7 *hammerhead shark*
8 *red snapper*
9 *California sea-lion*
10 *spotted eagle ray*
11 *Pacific octopus*
12 *puffer fish*
13 *moray eel*

The continental shelf marks the end of the shallows and the beginnings of deep water.

Blue spotted ray

Like most rays, this one spends much of its life on the seabed, making it hard for **predators** to spot. If attacked it can also defend itself with the two **venomous spines** in its tail.

Pacific lobster

This brightly coloured **scavenger** hides amongst rocks during the day. At night it comes out to feed on worms and other small animals.

Pacific octopus

This giant octopus can grow much bigger than a man! It can have up to a 9-metre (30-foot) arm-span, but is a very shy and gentle animal. Its favourite foods are crabs and lobsters.

The twilight zone

As we dive deeper down the continental slope things start to change. It gets much colder – our temperature **gauge** drops to 5°C (41°F). We are so deep we can hardly see any sunlight, so we switch on the **submersible's** lights.

There are far fewer fish down here, but our lights soon attract them. The deeper we go, the stranger the fish look. Many fish and shrimp here have what look like tiny headlights. They have special **organs** on their skin that produce light. These are used to identify and attract a **mate** or to attract **prey**. Some can "turn on" these lights in a sudden flash of brilliance to confuse a **predator**.

These squid have large eyes and light organs to help them see and be seen.

Hatchet fish

Most hunters in the twilight zone look upward to see if they can spot the dark shadow of another fish against the dim light from above. Hatchet fish have light organs along their belly and tail that make them glow just enough to match the light above them. Viewed from below the fish are almost invisible to predators. Like many fish in the twilight zone they swim upwards at night to feed in the richer, shallower waters when many predators are asleep.

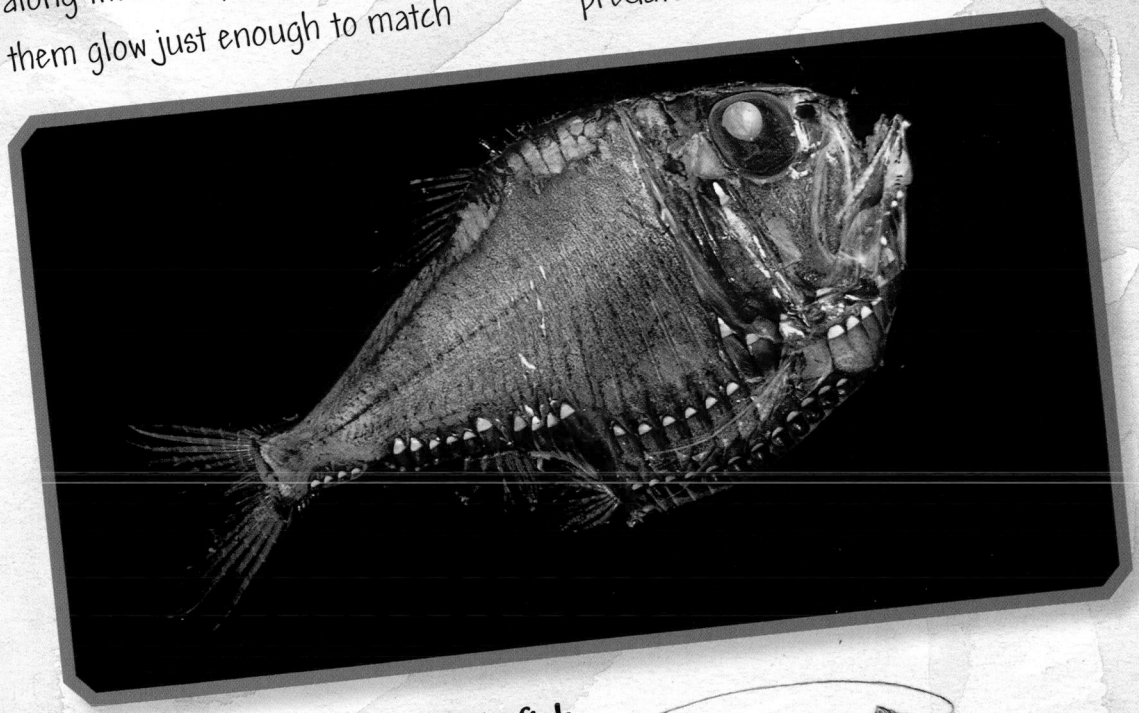

Viper fish

Like many twilight hunters these fish have huge jaws filled with large fangs and a special fin with a light on the end. This **lure** acts like a fishing rod, attracting smaller prey, which the viper fish gobbles up.

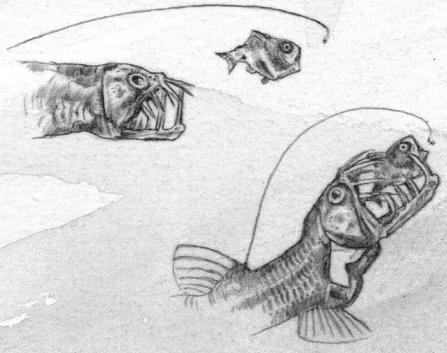

Deep water giants

We have been travelling down for over two hours now. Below 200 metres (650 feet) there is so little light that no seaweed or plant life can grow. Therefore there is no **plankton** down here. The fish feed on animal **carcasses** or droppings, falling down from above, or on each other.

Suddenly we pick up something huge on our **radar**. It is two sperm whales, diving straight down into the depths to feed. We peer out of the **porthole**. These incredible whales are shaped like submarines and can dive to amazing depths to hunt for their favourite **prey**, giant squid.

Sperm whales have tiny eyes but can find their prey in the darkness using **sonar**.

Whipnose

The whipnose uses its incredibly long **lure** to attract prey nearer and nearer to its hungry mouth.

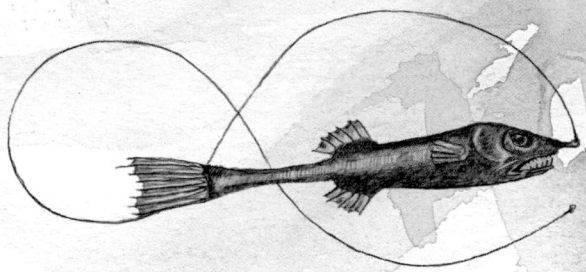

Sperm whale

The huge, blunt **snout** of the sperm whale acts like a heavy weight, helping it sink down quickly into the depths to hunt. The whale can hold its breath for over an hour!

Giant squid

These massive but mysterious animals can weigh over a tonne and reach lengths of over 16 metres (52 feet)! Dead bodies of these huge creatures have been washed onto beaches, but they have never been filmed alive.

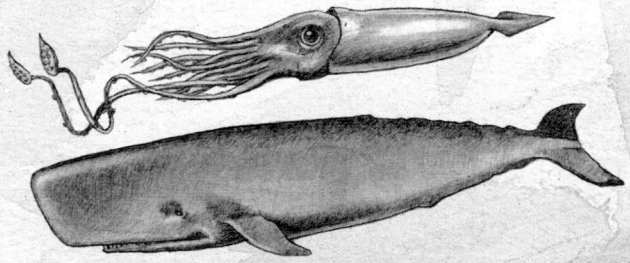

Into the darkness

We are very deep now – deeper than 1,000 metres (3,300 feet). The immense weight of the water above us presses down on the **titanium hull** of our **submersible**. This **pressure** would crush a diver like a paper cup. The water is nearly freezing, and there's no light. When we switch off the submersible's lights and look through the thick **plexiglass porthole** all we see is inky blackness. Down in this alien world many of the animals are completely blind. They are often coloured black, making them hard to see even with our lights back on. There is very little food down here. Hunters will attack and try to gobble up any fish they find, no matter what the size.

Many deep-sea fish, like this dragon fish, have a long thread called a lure which they use like a fishing rod to attract their **prey**.

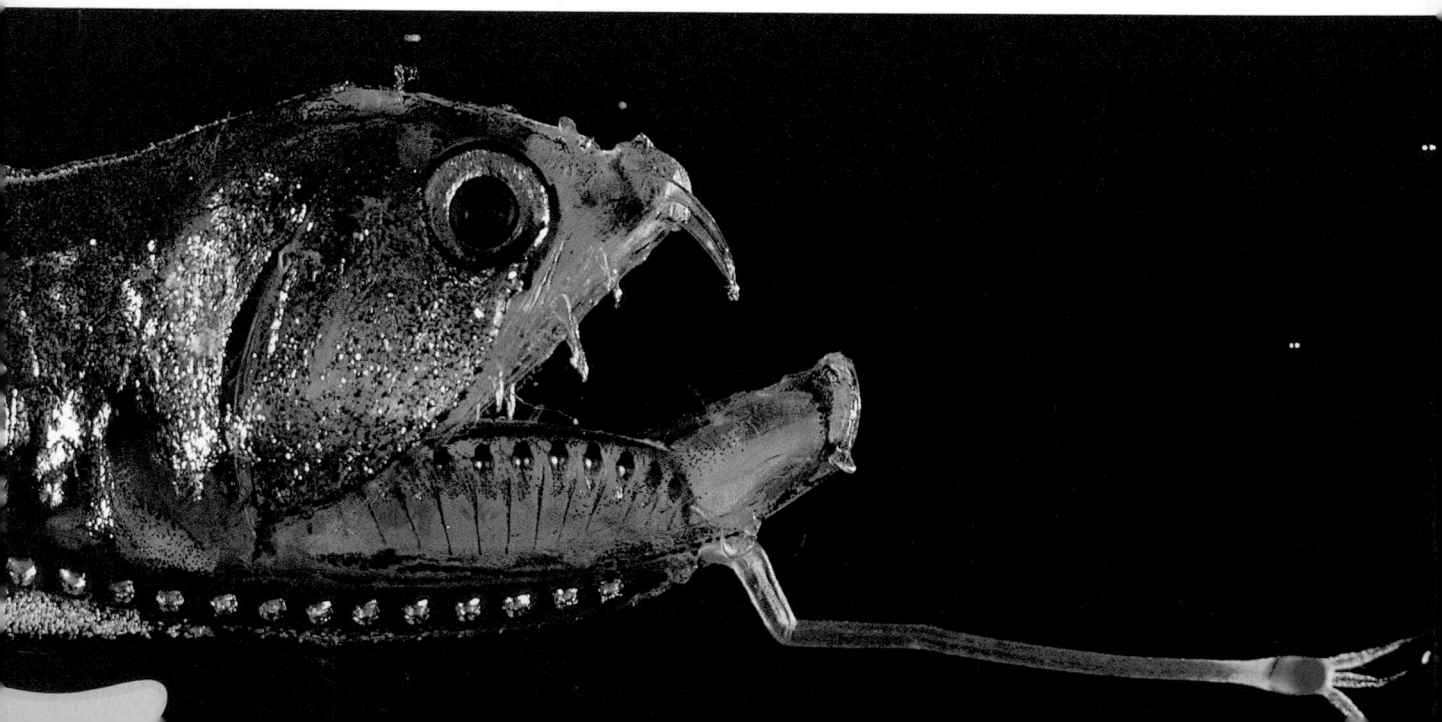

Fangtooth

The fangtooth's mouth bristles with huge teeth. It is also called an ogrefish – for obvious reasons!

Gulper eel

The gulper eel is like a giant swimming mouth. It drifts along until it meets another fish, then it opens its huge mouth and strikes.

Deep-sea angler

The female angler fish grows up to one metre (3.3 feet) long but the male is tiny. The male spends its life holding onto the female. She has a **lure** tipped with a light **organ** and a huge bag-like stomach that means she can eat fish up to twice her own size!

At the ocean floor

We are nearly 3,000 metres (10,000 feet) down now. The **hull** of the **submersible** creaks and groans under the enormous **pressure** above. The water outside is below freezing. Suddenly our lights pick up the ocean floor below.

The surface of the ocean floor is made up of the tiny skeletons and droppings of millions of animals. It forms a thick layer of mud that will stir up into a cloud if touched. There are no corals or clumps of seaweed. There are few signs of life here. It is like a desert. As we move along above the mud we start to see more and more snails and worms making their way slowly and carefully along the muddy ooze.

1 *deep-sea prawn*
2 *sea-cucumber*
3 *nudibranch*
4 *sea-urchin*
5 *sea-lilies*
6 *rat fish*
7 *halosaur*
8 *tripod fish*
9 *brittle star*

The deep-ocean floor is a still, barren desert.

Tripod fish

The special fins of this fish help it to "stand" above the ocean floor and wait to catch the **scent** of any food nearby.

Sea-spider

This strange blind creature is not a real spider. It walks along the muddy seabed on its long spindly legs, looking for worms to eat with its tube-like mouth.

Brittle star

These delicate starfish feed on tiny food **particles** they find on the seabed. If an attacker bites off one of their arms they can grow another.

The sulphur vents

Suddenly our temperature **gauge** starts to show warmer water. How could this be? We start to notice more fish. Then we discover the reason. Deep below us, water is being heated by hot **lava** and shooting up through cracks in the ocean floor. The water carries **minerals** through these cracks which form large **vents** on the seabed like chimneys. The water is also full of **sulphur**, which is eaten by bacteria. A whole **colony** of amazing animals lives around these chimneys, feeding on this bacteria.

Beyond us is another cliff-edge, leading to a deep-water trench. Even we cannot go any deeper. It is time to return to the surface. Who knows what creatures remain to be discovered in this amazing and wonderful world?

Huge worms and clams feed on the sulphur bacteria. Fish, crabs, shrimp, and thousands of anemones also live around the vents.

Tube worms

Huge red worms in long white tubes live around the chimneys. They grow up to one metre (3.3 feet) long.

A special world

Until these vents were discovered it was thought that all life on the planet needed the Sun to survive. Plants cannot grow without sunlight. Without plants, every other life form would die. The amazing thing about the sulphur vents is the animals here do not need sunlight to keep them alive.

Giant clams

Giant 30-cm (12-inch) long white clams also live around the vents.

Conservation and the future

Pollution

For years people have treated the oceans like a huge sewer. It was thought that the seas were so big and so deep you could throw anything you want into them and it would be washed away. Sewage, rubbish, and industrial waste such as petroleum and insecticides were pumped or dumped straight into the sea. Recently scientists have realized that pollutants do enormous damage in the sea. Many chemicals get eaten by tiny sea creatures which are then eaten by fish – and finally by people!

Now many countries have laws to control and stop ocean pollution, but a huge amount of sea dumping still occurs.

Captains of oil tankers still dump huge amounts of unwanted oil into the sea, killing thousands of sea birds.

Over-fishing

Many of the fish and whales in the sea have been hunted by humans almost to **extinction**. Modern fishing boats have **sonar** to find the fish and huge nets to catch whole **shoals**. Many larger animals such as dolphins and sharks are also caught and killed in these nets by accident. Many countries are trying to control this over-fishing. Most whale-hunting has now been banned, but it may be too late for some species of whale, such as the beluga.

One new idea is to create **marine**-protected areas where no one can pollute or kill the wildlife. These nature reserves are one of many ways we can preserve marine wildlife for the future.

The most famous marine-protected area is the Great Barrier Reef Marine Park in Australia.

Glossary

carcass	dead body (usually of an animal)
colony	group of similar things living together
continental shelf	shallow area of seabed between the land and the depths of the water
current	a movement of water, sometimes caused by the tide
extinction	when a type of animal or plant dies out and will never live again
fry	young fish
gauge	instrument for measuring or testing something
gorge	very deep, steep valley cut into the ground by a river
hull	the frame of a boat or ship
larva	(more than one = larvae) an insect just after it is born
lava	hot, melting rock that comes out of cracks in the Earth
lone	only, or on its own
lure	something that lights up on a fish's head so it can attract prey
marine	to do with the sea
mate	when a male and a female come together to have babies
migrate	to move from one place to another, often to feed or mate
mineral	a natural substance, that usually comes from the ground, such as salt
organ	part of a body that does a job to make the body work
particle	very small piece of something
plankton	tiny animal and plant life that floats or swims in water

plexiglass	very strong, see-through plastic
porthole	window in the side of a ship
predator	animal that hunts, kills, and eats other animals
pressure	the weight of something pressing or being pressed
prey	animals that are eaten by predators
propeller	blade that turns quickly to help a vehicle move forward
radar	way of finding things using radio waves
scavenger	something that looks for and feeds on leftovers
scent	smell
shoal	large group of the same type of fish
snout	animal's nose
sonar	(SOund and NAvigation Ranging) a way of finding objects, especially underwater, using sound waves
spawn	when water animals lay many eggs together
spine	a special stiff or pointed fish fin
submersible	underwater craft used for deep-sea research
sulphur	a chemical element (also spelt sulfur)
tentacle	a long and flexible part of some animals that is used to feel and touch
titanium	a silver-grey, light but strong, metal
venomous	poisonous
vent	opening for gas or liquid to escape from

Find out more

Further reading

Adapted for Success: Sharks and other fish, Andrew Solway (Heinemann Library, 2006)

Biomes Atlases: Oceans and Beaches, Trevor Day (Raintree, 2003)

Food Chains and Webs: Ocean Food Chains, Emma Lynch (Heinemann Library, 2005)

Sea Creatures: Sharks, Carol Baldwin (Heinemann Library, 2003)

Organizations

Earthwatch

267 Banbury Road

Oxford

OX2 7HT

www.earthwatch.org

Friends of the Earth

26–28 Underwood Street

London N1 2PN

www.foe.co.uk

Marine Conservation Society
Unit 3 Wolf Business Park
Alton Road
Ross-on-Wye
Herefordshire
HR9 5NB
www.mcsuk.org

Using the Internet

If you want to find out more about oceans, you can go to one of the website addresses below. Alternatively, you can use a search engine, such as www.yahooligans.com or www.internet4kids.com, and type in a keyword such as "ocean", or a related subject such as "submersibles".

Websites

www.bbc.co.uk/nature/blueplanet/games.shtml

This page of the BBC website includes games based on information from the website's sea-life section.

www.sanctuaries.nos.noaa.gov/oms/oms.html

The US government's official National Oceanic and Atmospheric Administration (NOAA) website features a clickable map and profiles of many protected ocean areas.

Index

abyss 9
angler fish 21
clams 24, 25
conservation 27
continental shelf 8, 14
continental slope 8, 14
dark zone 9, 20
dragon fish 20
eels 14, 21
flying fish 11
Great Barrier Reef Marine Park 27
hatchet fish 17
krill 12
lobsters 15
Marianas Trench 7
near shore zone 8, 10
ocean floor 9, 22, 24
ocean trenches 7, 9, 24
octopus 14, 15
over-fishing 27
Pacific Ocean 6, 7
plankton 12, 13
pollution 26
Portuguese man o' war 11
predators 10, 11, 15, 16, 17, 19, 20, 21
rays 10, 12, 14, 15
sailfish 11
salmon 13
sea-spider 23
sharks 12, 13, 14, 27
squid 16, 18, 19, 21
starfish 22, 23
sulphur vents 9, 24, 25
sunlit zone 8, 9, 12
tripod fish 22, 23
tube worms 24, 25
twilight zone 8, 9, 16, 17
viper fish 17
whales 12, 18, 19, 27
whipnose 19